Who Needs A Career Coach Anyway?

The Ultimate Tell-All And Dream Career Navigation Guide To Take You From Where You Are – To Where You're Meant To Be.

BY LAKRISHA DAVIS

© 2018 Lakrisha Davis & Co.

Copyright © 2018 All rights reserved.

This book or any portion thereof may not be reproduced or used in any manner whatsoever without the express written permission of the author.

This book is licensed for your personal enjoyment only. No part of this book may be reproduced or transmitted in any form or by any means, electronic or mechanical, including photocopying, recording or by any information storage and retrieval system, without permission of the author.

Thank you for respecting the proprietary work of the author.

ISBN-13: 978-0-692-10894-9
Published by Lakrisha Davis & Co

TABLE OF CONTENTS

CHAPTER ONE
Introduction:
Setting the Scene
PAGE 1

CHAPTER TWO
Career Exploration:
Defining Your Dream Job
PAGE 9

CHAPTER THREE
The Hidden Treasure:
The Truth About Cover Letters
PAGE 16

CHAPTER FOUR
Job Navigation Tool:
Writing a Resume That WORKS
PAGE 21

CHAPTER FIVE
My Job Search Roadmap:
Smart (Not Hard) Job Hunting
PAGE 34

CHAPTER SIX
Sink or Sail?
Working Effectively with Recruiters
PAGE 45

TABLE OF CONTENTS
(CONTINUED)

CHAPTER SEVEN
The "Resumes Are Dead" Way:
Networking to the Offer
PAGE 53

CHAPTER EIGHT
Destination LinkedIn:
Leveraging LinkedIn In Your Job Search
PAGE 61

CHAPTER NINE
Cruising the Interview:
Becoming an Interviewing Pro
PAGE 74

CHAPTER TEN
Bumps in the Road:
Lessons About Age Discrimination
PAGE 90

CHAPTER ELEVEN
Hitting a Goldmine:
Negotiating the Offer
PAGE 98

For the job seeker who's
freshly on the job market...
transitioning careers...
or returning to the
workforce.

"ONE DAY, OR DAY ONE? YOU DECIDE."

—UNKNOWN

CHAPTER I
INTRODUCTION
SETTING THE SCENE

Once Upon a Time, job hunting was as simple as applying for a few positions online (or in person), going on job interviews, and accepting a new role. Today, we live in a job market where companies now use applicant tracking systems to screen resumes; they increasingly hire from within their primary networks; and candidates could sometimes go on 3 to 4 interviews with a company and still not get the job. We also have a hidden job market of opportunities that job seekers can only uncover through networking. Hiring moves a lot slower than the older days, and the recruiting industry has markedly changed, too. So, before we get into all the mechanics of how to land your dream career, we should first discuss some important factors about the evolution of the job market, along with a few job search rules, that every job seeker should know from the very onset.

The Fall of Online Job Applications

Let's start with something that's out of everyone's control. More and more companies fill roles internally and give secondary candidates less rank among internal applicants, or people that their employees know. "Is it better to build from within, or 'buy' from the external job market?" "Are people that our employees can vouch for more likely to thrive or flame out?" Hiring statistics show that 85% of the time, job seekers land the best careers strictly through networking – and that companies publish only approximately 70-80% of their jobs online. Consequently, job seekers that focus solely on online job applications miss out on a wealth of available opportunities. To survive the modern-day hiring climate, job seekers must think outside of the box, use social media, attend networking events, or join professional organizations.

Applicant Tracking Systems Exist

Back then, a real human with hiring power would screen candidate resumes. Now, companies use Applicant Tracking Systems (ATS) to assist with their recruitment needs, which has drastically changed the way of resume writing. The systems help hiring managers quickly sort through qualified vs. unqualified candidates based on keywords scanned on their profiles.

A Candidate-Driven Job Market

Interestingly, on one hand, employers say that it's hard to find good talent, while on the other, job seekers say that it's hard to land good job opportunities. But, the job market has greatly changed since the Great Recession, and we now live in a candidate-driven market. Compared to 2008, or even just a few years ago, candidates possess far more power in their careers than ever before—especially professionals with skills that are in short supply or who work in industries that have grown post-recession. So, ultimately, your career is up to you.

We live in an age of increased visibility of information, where online sources show reviews of companies before you interview, or you can easily find information about emerging industries to apply for jobs that really make an impact. Recruiters are also excellent resources to get insider information about a company's culture or structure. In short, the days of candidates feeling thankful simply for having a job are null and void, as they can now call the shots in their careers.

Never Fall in Love with a Lead

Never put all your faith into one single job opportunity, or allow interviews (including successful ones) to put a pause on your job search. In this market, nothing's ever final until the company has tendered a written offer; it's signed or agreed upon by both parties; and you've received an official start date. Falling in love with leads and quitting your job search before you officially receive an offer greatly puts you at risk of losing out on other great opportunities just for a "strong possibility". Remember, things sometimes happen beyond our control; companies put positions on hold and companies may like you, yet still go with another candidate. Even when recruiters or friends guarantee you that they could "get you in" somewhere, don't put all your eggs in one basket until there's a signed offer on the table.

Let Go of How Things "Should" Be

"When I argue with reality, I lose - but only 100 percent of the time."
– Byron Katie

Many could argue that the hiring practices of the 21st Century make it extremely difficult for people to find jobs. But the reality is, right here and right now, you are on the job market. Thinking, "This sucks because of...," or "Dream jobs don't exist," or "Recruiters never give feedback," or "Companies shouldn't interview people if they're just going to hire internally anyways," only creates unnecessary friction. Pain gets our attention, so it's easy to get caught up in what sucks about a situation. But with the right effort, you can always find some positive elements — that is, if you take notice of what you need to learn from your negative experiences.

Turn your letdowns into ambition instead of inaction, and spend time learning from your mistakes. Try looking at your efforts positively rather than resorting to self-criticism about unsuccessful interviews, or a quiet month with respect to your resume. Focus less on the problems that occur, and more on possible solutions. For example, if you're not getting called for interviews, check your resume. Or, hone the necessary skills to make you more desirable to your target companies. Understand that you will not get every job you apply for and that you may need to learn some hard lessons before landing the right opportunity.

INTRODUCTION

"Maybe you weren't rejected; you were divinely redirected!"

—Unknown

It's Never Personal

Here's the final and probably the most important rule you need to know about job hunting: never take it personally. Companies put their businesses first and make decisions based on what they feel aligns the most with their business needs. Their hiring methods, or who they ultimately choose to hire, have nothing to do with you, personally. I know that it's hard to stay encouraged if you've gone on countless interviews, or sent out hundreds of resumes. But, remember, it only takes one. Somewhere, a hiring manager is looking for someone just like you!

"TOO MANY OF US ARE NOT LIVING OUR DREAMS BECAUSE WE'RE LIVING OUR FEARS."

—LES BROWN

CHAPTER II
CAREER EXPLORATION:
DEFINING YOUR DREAM JOB

By now, you've heard about a dozen times that you need to tailor your efforts during your job search. However, this doesn't end with settling on job titles to target. If you're in search for your dream job, you must clearly and specifically define what that means to you... what the culture looks like...and how you'll spend your day. It's important to be able to articulate your dream job. Our greatest power comes from doing things we love, following our passions, and using our best talents. We spend one-third of our lives at work and deserve to feel fulfilled by it. But the catch is, your success in landing your dream career entirely depends on your own ability to define what a "dream job" means to you.

Create your dream job description:

- *State your position title:*
- *What does your dream company stand for?*
- *List your main responsibilities:*
- *Describe how you spend your day.*
- *How are you rewarded for your work?*
- *What is your salary?*
- *How does your job fit into your personal life?*

These aspirations make a good starting point, but it's more important to know what skills you'll need, and how to build them. A career roadmap lays the path to your ultimate dream job. It helps you examine how closely your career history aligns with your goals. You can't map your route if you don't know your destination.

So, for your first step in planning your dream career, create a detailed inventory of your skills and accomplishments. Then, complete a profile of the ideal candidate for the role you're seeking, as hiring managers would describe it. And finally, make note of any existing gaps in your skill- or experience level that you need to work towards filling (if any).

ACCOMPLISHMENTS - Career History

INDUSTRIES	I.	II.	III.
Functional Areas (e.g. HR, Finance, Marketing)			
Former Titles			
Competencies/ Skills Gained			

CAREER EXPLORATION

ASPIRING - Career Goals

INDUSTRIES	I.	II.	III.
Target Roles			
Top Job Compentencies /Requirements			
Relevant Historical Skills & Experience			
Competency Gaps			
Experience Gaps			
Personal Qualities (relevant to the industry)			

Are there any specific or significant gaps in my background/ experience?

_____

_____

_____

What is the best fit for the service I can offer and occupations that deliver it?

_____

_____

_____

When I feel the happiest or inspired, what am I doing?

_____

_____

_____

What is my list of non-negotiables based on my past roles/ experiences?

_____

_____

_____

"IF OPPORTUNITY DOESN'T KNOCK, BUILD A DOOR."

—MILTON BERLE

CHAPTER III
THE HIDDEN TREASURE:
THE TRUTH ABOUT COVER LETTERS

There are so many conflicting opinions about cover letters. Some people question whether hiring managers even bother to read them, or if cover letters could really increase a person's candidacy for the job. Well, the truth is, not all hiring managers read cover letters. Some hiring managers (1) disregard them completely, (2) appreciate the gesture but still toss them, or (3) take offense to candidates who skip this step entirely. So, since you never know who you'll get, it's best to cover yourself in any case. Cover letters don't take a ton of time, anyway, and shouldn't exceed more than one page. Truthfully, tailoring your resume for every position takes more time than doing a cover letter.

Think of cover letters as the 'laser pointer' to highlight exactly why you're the perfect candidate for the job. A good cover letter is not about you, although it seems that way because you're writing about yourself. It's about the job the company wants to fill and how you meet the requirements. Most people fail to realize this and just use the cover letter as an opportunity to regurgitate everything that's in their resumes. And while there's a host of things that make hiring professionals cringe when reading cover letters, going on and on about all your accomplishments certainly makes the list. You also double up on useless information and miss out on a huge opportunity to showcase other skills or outside experience that might not be on your resume but are perfect for the position. However, with a customizable cover letter, you get the chance to add some extra keywords, as there's a good chance that a software program will be reading your letter first before it's screened by the hiring manager.

The "shopping cart" cover letter proves an effective way to evidence that you're the perfect candidate for the position. It starts out with an opening paragraph to express your interest in the opportunity. Then the central paragraph, rather than a story style paragraph, highlights exactly what the employer is looking for, along with your own matching qualifications. Pretend that the employer is going to the grocery store to shop for their "Dream Candidate." It's up to you to use the job description to fill the company's shopping cart. Finally, the concluding paragraph ends the letter with a call-to-action.

COVER LETTER EXAMPLE

YOUR NAME
City, State | (555) 555-5555 | youremail@gmail.com | www.linkedin.com/in/linkedinrul

Today's Date

Hiring Manager
Company Name
City, State
Posting ID#

RE: **Position Title***

I am an achievement-oriented professional with extensive experience in _____, _____ and _____. I recently learned about this vacancy within your organization and wanted to inquire about the possibility of joining your team. With a proven track record of excellence, and a list of highly specialized skills, I believe that I would make an excellent fit. I would like to officially apply for the **Position Title*** position with **Insert Company Name***.

In my most recent position with _____, I successfully *** insert key career highlight.**

At this stage in my career, I am eager to locate a new challenging position where I can continue to offer my leadership skills and provide a positive impact. I understand that the **Position Title*** will **Insert Key Responsibility**. Regarding the position's requirements, I have:

- Key Requirement #1
- Key Requirement #2
- Key Requirement #3
- Key Requirement #4

After reviewing the responsibilities and requirements of this position, I am confident that I make an outstanding candidate. I would greatly appreciate the opportunity to discuss this position further. You may contact me via the information provided at your earliest convenience. I look forward to hearing from you and appreciate your consideration in advance.

Best regards,

Your Name

Enclosure: Resume

This easily customizable, 'shopping cart' cover letter allows you to pull in qualifications directly from the job description.

"EVERY EXIT IS AN ENTRANCE TO A NEW EXPERIENCE."

—UNKNOWN

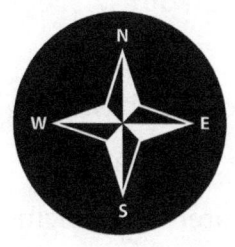

CHAPTER IV
JOB NAVIGATION TOOL:
WRITING A RESUME THAT WORKS

The first thing you should know about resume writing is that your resume isn't about you; it's about what you can do. The only way you'll work is if your resume works. When resumes don't work, usually it's because the resume (1) isn't discoverable by hiring managers in applicant tracking systems, and/or (2) doesn't tell a story based on the target position. The best way to begin the process of writing your resume is to first establish the 1 to 3 job target titles that you want to target during your job search. This sets the structure for your entire resume strategy — from the format to choose, the keywords to include, and more.

Raising Your Discoverability

You increase your visibility to hiring managers in applicant tracking systems by choosing the right keywords and content to include in your resume. Research is key when constructing your resume because you'll need to anticipate the keywords recruiters will be looking to find in the database of resumes. When recruiters source for candidates, they look to ATS to bring them the most qualified people for the job. Typically, resumes containing the most keywords, qualifications, or skills stand a better chance at beating the algorithms in ATS.

Writing Your Story

You need to focus on telling a clear and concise story based on the target job description(s). Companies don't care about everything you've ever done; companies only care whether you can perform the job successfully. Most people think about their day to day job duties, problems they've solved, or daily activities when writing their resumes. This often confuses job seekers about the information that truly belongs on their resumes, or, what defines "under" and "over-selling." It's best to focus on information that directly qualifies you for the position based on the job description. Study your target description(s) to get an idea about how hiring managers think about, describe, and prioritize your target role(s). Then, go back and look at your own history of work to pull out experiences that best reflect you can do the job.

Be sure to include relevant and specific accomplishments or quantifiable achievements on your resume (e.g. revenue increases, improved efficiencies, reduced costs, or other leadership contributions). Also, think about projects or programs you've worked on, or initiatives you helped to advance. This is what companies care the most about your story. Sure, they want to know about your skillset, but would much rather know whether you've been successful in the use of those skills. For job results that you can't quantify, talk about the overall value you brought to an organization from certain projects or initiatives—such as improving the team's culture, or revamping processes. Don't limit yourself by thinking in terms of the day-to-day, and start thinking about your value-adds on a much grander scale. Instead of just using words, demonstrate how you used that skill.

Choosing a Resume Type

It's important to choose the perfect resume style that best flaunts your relevant skills and experiences for the job. There are 3 common resume types: chronological, functional, and combination. And, they each serve different purposes.

The most commonly used format is the chronological resume, which best suits individuals whose work history is stable and professional growth is consistent within a field. The chronological format is exactly what it sounds like: it follows your work history backward from the current job, detailing companies, dates, and responsibilities.

Functional resumes focus on your most qualified skills and accomplishments for the position, but de-emphasizes when, where, or how you got that experience. This format is especially my favorite for candidates changing careers, returning to work after an absence, or entering the workforce out of college. The functional resume should emphasize the most relevant experience to the job, while de-emphasizing jobs, employment dates, and job titles.

Finally, the combination resume is a format that best suits professionals with demonstrated growth and continued progression within an industry or profession. It often starts with a performance profile, then lists job-specific skills or accomplishments, and segues into a chronological format that lists how and when these skills were attained.

Bringing It All Together: Planning Your Resume Sections

Contact Information

For contact information, be sure to include all the details your reader needs to know to reach you: your first and last name, city and state, phone number, email, and the link to your LinkedIn profile. (Note: If you're considering relocation, leave your city/state off altogether).

Target Position + Brand Statement

You need to state a target job title (i.e. "Human Resources Executive") so that your career intent is clearly identifiable. A branding statement could also give support to the brand you're presenting and let readers know what they can expect from you.

Career/Professional Summary

An objective statement robs you of the credibility you deserve, plus, hiring managers will likely skip over it. Instead of an objective statement, use a Professional Summary to demonstrate why you're the best person for the job. Your summary should resonate the high-caliber skill-sets and talents you've got to offer, and entice readers to want to continue learning about you.

Core Competencies

What are the major buzzwords or keywords in your industry that hiring managers search for in the database of resumes? Familiarize yourself with these words, and list between 9 to 12 competencies on your resume. This gives you the opportunity to highlight core skills that don't fit in the body of your resume. Repeat these keywords in the context of each job to further increase your visibility in the search database.

Work Experience

Your work details must focus directly on the target job description(s). Remember to collect a few job descriptions and go through each of them, bullet point by bullet point, to learn how companies describe your target position(s). If you're switching industries, make sure that you pay close attention to transferable skills.

Additional Experience

In this section, state any additional experience that's relevant to the job—listing the title and organization only. When you think of this section, picture related job experience dated past 10-12 years, volunteer work, professional associations, internships and other experience you'd like to reserve as talking points for interviews.

Education

The first rule of thumb for detailing educational experience on your resume is to ensure that you know the correct way to list your degrees, certifications, or trainings. Also, if your concentration or major isn't relevant to your career pursuits now, you can leave it off. For instance, if you're now an accountant but studied English, simply state "Bachelor of Arts Degree" instead of "Bachelor of Arts in English" for your degree. As a final note, whether you are a millennial or seasoned worker, don't include graduation dates for discrimination reasons.

JOB NAVIGATION TOOL

SAMPLE COMBINATION RESUME

YOUR NAME

Street Address ♦ Phone Number ♦ Email Address

TARGET JOB TITLE/BRANDING STATEMENT

Keyword#1 / Keyword#2 / Keyword#3 / Keyword#4 / Keyword#5 / Keyword#6 / Keyword#7 / Keyword#8 / Keyword#9 Keyword#10 / Keyword#11 / Keyword#12 / Keyword#13 / Keyword#14 / Keyword#15 /

This is my career summary. This is my career summary.

SELECTED CONTRIBUTIONS

- This was a key contribution. This was a key contribution. This was a key contribution. This was a key contribution.
- This was a key contribution. This was a key contribution. This was a key contribution. This was a key contribution.
- This was a key contribution. This was a key contribution. This was a key contribution. This was a key contribution.
- This was a key contribution. This was a key contribution. This was a key contribution. This was a key contribution.
- This was a key contribution. This was a key contribution. This was a key contribution. This was a key contribution.
- This was a key contribution. This was a key contribution. This was a key contribution. This was a key contribution.
- This was a key contribution. This was a key contribution. This was a key contribution. This was a key contribution.

PROFESSIONAL EXPERIENCE

JOB TITLE   00/0000 – 00/0000
Company Name – City, State
These are my core responsibilities/functions/job activities. These are my core responsibilities/functions/job activities. These are my core responsibilities/functions/job activities. These are my core responsibilities/functions/job activities. These are my core responsibilities/functions/job activities.

JOB TITLE   00/0000 – 00/0000
Company Name – City, State
These are my core responsibilities/functions/job activities. These are my core responsibilities/functions/job activities. These are my core responsibilities/functions/job activities. These are my core responsibilities/functions/job activities.

JOB TITLE   00/0000 – 00/0000
Company Name – City, State
These are my core responsibilities/functions/job activities. These are my core responsibilities/functions/job activities. These are my core responsibilities/functions/job activities. These are my core responsibilities/functions/job activities.

JOB TITLE   00/0000 – 00/0000
Company Name – City, State
These are my core responsibilities/functions/job activities. These are my core responsibilities/functions/job activities. These are my core responsibilities/functions/job activities. These are my core responsibilities/functions/job activities.

EDUCATION

DEGREE NAME
Institution Name – City, State

A sample combination resume, which usually serves as a consolidated resume for executive professionals - or the resume format for job seekers without a progressive career record in a given field.

WHO NEEDS A CAREER COACH ANYWAY?

SAMPLE CHRONOLOGICAL RESUME

YOUR NAME

City, State | (555) 555-5555 | youremail@gmail.com | www.linkedin.com/in/linkedinrul

TARGET JOB TITLE/BRANDING STATEMENT

This is my career summary. This is my career summary.

Professional Strengths Include:

Keyword#1 | Keyword#2 | Keyword#3 | Keyword#4 | Keyword#5 | Keyword#6 | Keyword#7 | Keyword#8
Keyword#9 | Keyword#10 | Keyword#11 | Keyword#12 | Keyword#13 | Keyword#14 | Keyword#15

PROFESSIONAL EXPERIENCE

JOB TITLE   00/0000 – present
Company Name – City, State

- These are my core responsibilities/job activities. These are my core responsibilities/functions/job activities.
- These are my core responsibilities/job activities. These are my core responsibilities/functions/job activities.
- These are my core responsibilities/functions/job activities. These are my core responsibilities/job activities.
- These are my core responsibilities/job activities. These are my core responsibilities/functions/job activities.
- These are my core responsibilities/job activities. These are my core responsibilities/functions/job activities.
- These are my core responsibilities/job activities. These are my core responsibilities/functions/job activities.

JOB TITLE   00/0000 – 00/0000
Company Name – City, State

- These are my core responsibilities/job activities. These are my core responsibilities/functions/job activities.
- These are my core responsibilities/job activities. These are my core responsibilities/functions/job activities.
- These are my core responsibilities/job activities. These are my core responsibilities/functions/job activities.
- These are my core responsibilities/job activities. These are my core responsibilities/functions/job activities.
- These are my core responsibilities/job activities. These are my core responsibilities/functions/job activities.

JOB TITLE   00/0000 – 00/0000
Company Name – City, State

- These are my core responsibilities/job activities. These are my core responsibilities/functions/job activities.
- These are my core responsibilities/job activities. These are my core responsibilities/functions/job activities.
- These are my core responsibilities/job activities. These are my core responsibilities/functions/job activities.
- These are my core responsibilities/job activities. These are my core responsibilities/functions/job activities.
- These are my core responsibilities/job activities. These are my core responsibilities/functions/job activities.

ADDITIONAL EXPERIENCE

JOB TITLE   00/0000 – present
Company Name – City, State

EDUCATION

DEGREE NAME
Institution Name – City, State

The most commonly used resume format (chronological resume) for professionals with a progressive career record in a specific role or industry.

JOB NAVIGATION TOOL

SAMPLE ACCOMPLISHMENT CHRONOLOGICAL RESUME

YOUR NAME

City, State | (555) 555-5555 | youremail@gmail.com | www.linkedin.com/in/linkedinrul

TARGET JOB TITLE/BRANDING STATEMENT

This is my career summary. This is my career summary.

CORE COMPETENCIES

CORE COMPETENCY #1	CORE COMPETENCY #2	CORE COMPETENCY #3
CORE COMPETENCY #4	CORE COMPETENCY #5	CORE COMPETENCY #6
CORE COMPETENCY #7	CORE COMPETENCY #8	CORE COMPETENCY #9

PROFESSIONAL EXPERIENCE

JOB TITLE 00/0000 – present
Company Name – City, State

These are my core responsibilities/functions/job activities. These are my core responsibilities/functions/job activities. These are my core responsibilities/functions/job activities. These are my core responsibilities/functions/job activities. These are my core responsibilities/functions/job activities.

Key Contributions:

- This was a key contribution. This was a key contribution. This was a key contribution. This was a key contribution.
- This was a key contribution. This was a key contribution. This was a key contribution. This was a key contribution.
- This was a key contribution. This was a key contribution. This was a key contribution. This was a key contribution.

JOB TITLE 00/0000 – 00/0000
Company Name – City, State

These are my core responsibilities/functions/job activities. These are my core responsibilities/functions/job activities. These are my core responsibilities/functions/job activities. These are my core responsibilities/functions/job activities. These are my core responsibilities/functions/job activities.

Key Contributions:

- This was a key contribution. This was a key contribution. This was a key contribution. This was a key contribution.
- This was a key contribution. This was a key contribution. This was a key contribution. This was a key contribution.
- This was a key contribution. This was a key contribution. This was a key contribution. This was a key contribution.

JOB TITLE 00/0000 – 00/0000
Company Name – City, State

These are my core responsibilities/functions/job activities. These are my core responsibilities/functions/job activities. These are my core responsibilities/functions/job activities. These are my core responsibilities/functions/job activities. These are my core responsibilities/functions/job activities.

Key Contributions:

- This was a key contribution. This was a key contribution. This was a key contribution. This was a key contribution.
- This was a key contribution. This was a key contribution. This was a key contribution. This was a key contribution.
- This was a key contribution. This was a key contribution. This was a key contribution. This was a key contribution.

EDUCATION

DEGREE NAME
Institution Name – City, State

Chronological resume sample for professionals with plentiful quantifiable achievements.

SAMPLE FUNCTIONAL RESUME

YOUR NAME

Street Address ♦ Phone Number ♦ Email Address

TARGET JOB TITLE/BRANDING STATEMENT

This is my career summary. This is my career summary. This is my career summary. This is my career summary. This is my career summary. This is my career summary. This is my career summary. This is my career summary. This is my career summary. This is my career summary. This is my career summary. This is my career summary. This is my career summary. This is my career summary. This is my career summary. This is my career summary. This is my career summary. This is my career summary. This is my career summary.

Skills & Abilities

Keyword#1	Keyword#2	Keyword#3	Keyword#4
Keyword#5	Keyword#6	Keyword#7	Keyword#8
Keyword#9	Keyword#10	Keyword#11	Keyword#12
Keyword#13	Keyword#14	Keyword#15	Keyword#16

EDUCATION

DEGREE NAME 0000
Institution Name – City, State

Relevant Coursework: Relevant Course Name 1; Relevant Course Name 2; Relevant Course Name 3; Relevant Course Name 3; Relevant Course Name 4; Relevant Course Name 5

SUMMARY OF QUALIFICATIONS

- This was a qualification I gained through college/internships/volunteer experience/real-world experiences.
- This was a qualification I gained through college/internships/volunteer experience/real-world experiences.
- This was a qualification I gained through college/internships/volunteer experience/real-world experiences.
- This was a qualification I gained through college/internships/volunteer experience/real-world experiences.
- This was a qualification I gained through college/internships/volunteer experience/real-world experiences.

CAREER HISTORY

JOB TITLE 00/0000 – 00/0000
Company Name – City, State
These are my core responsibilities/functions/job activities. These are my core responsibilities/functions/job activities. These are my core responsibilities/functions/job activities. These are my core responsibilities/functions/job activities.

JOB TITLE 00/0000 – 00/0000
Company Name – City, State
These are my core responsibilities/functions/job activities. These are my core responsibilities/functions/job activities. These are my core responsibilities/functions/job activities. These are my core responsibilities/functions/job activities.

JOB TITLE 00/0000 – 00/0000
Company Name – City, State
These are my core responsibilities/functions/job activities. These are my core responsibilities/functions/job activities. These are my core responsibilities/functions/job activities. These are my core responsibilities/functions/job activities.

JOB TITLE 00/0000 – 00/0000
Company Name – City, State
These are my core responsibilities/functions/job activities. These are my core responsibilities/functions/job activities. These are my core responsibilities/functions/job activities. These are my core responsibilities/functions/job activities.

The functional resume…most used by recent graduates or transitioning career professionals.

"IT'S NOT WHAT YOU ACHIEVE, IT'S WHAT YOU OVERCOME. THAT'S WHAT DEFINES YOUR CAREER."

—CARLTON FISK

CHAPTER V
MY JOB SEARCH ROADMAP:
SMART (NOT HARD) JOB HUNTING

The typical job search lifecycle begins with a resume update, and simply ends in submitting online applications with hopes of getting calls for interviews. However, in today's job market, job seekers run the risk of prolonging their job hunts precipitously, or burning themselves out, when they don't have the right execution strategy. Successful job hunting isn't just about your resume - the number of applications you submit - or the number of hours you spend performing your job search. What's important is that you (1) have a plan, (2) focus on quality rather than quantity, and (3) use other search methods than just applying for jobs online. Contrary to popular belief, job hunting is NOT "a full-time job in itself." If you're job hunting smart and not hard, you only spend 2 hours per day (max) performing your job search. Though a frustrating process, you'll certainly experience less of a headache by having the right strategies to help you navigate the process.

Job Boards

Decide on the job boards you want to focus on during your search. The most popular include Linkedin, Indeed, Career Builder, Monster, and now even Google and Facebook. But, don't neglect industry-specific sites, like, job boards exclusive for nonprofit or marketing professionals, for example. Be sure to create a candidate profile on the sites and set up your job alerts, if desired.

Set a Schedule

The first thing that you need to do when shaping your job search strategy is determine a schedule. For instance, what specific days and times are you able to job hunt?

Is it better for you to set aside, let's say, 1-hour per day to conduct your job search? Or, is committing yourself to 1 to 2 days out of the week for a few hours each day better for your current set of priorities or tolerance level? Again, the goal is quality over quantity. So, even if you're applying to just 2 to 3 jobs per day, that's good activity.

Pro Tip: *During your idle time, surf the job boards and flag positions to apply for later so you can get right to the application process when you do apply for jobs.*

Job Tracking

You'll need some form of tracking system to record, monitor, and assess your job search activity. Your job tracker should list the position's title, your application date, salary compensation, and information for a hiring contact to follow up with. The application date is important because you'll need to know when to follow up on your job submissions. It's obvious why you need to list the job title, but as for compensation, this gives insight into what the seat is paying, and whether the opportunity is something you'll be truly interested in.

Also, include the link to the job description for easy access.

Follow-up Method

The follow-up method is a huge area of opportunity for most job seekers. No response does not always mean "no," and job seekers that follow up on their applications go above and beyond to show their level of interest towards the job. Following up once saved my job search as a job seeker, and that's why I incorporated this step into my program for clients. In retrospect, I had quit my job without having a back-up plan, and couldn't leave all my faith in just submitting online applications. Well, that worked out very well for me. So, my advice for you is to simply designate 1 to 2 days out of the week to follow up on the prior week's submissions. Immediately after applying for a position, record it on your job search tracker so that on your follow-up days, you aren't scrambling to find hiring contacts.

The follow-up technique involves research. And for this reason, LinkedIn and Google will be your very best friends during your job search. Using the advanced people finder on LinkedIn, you can find hiring contacts to send InMails on the status of your applications. Or, search the company's Linkedin page and view all its employees that are on LinkedIn and source for hiring contacts that way. Since the number of results that you receive depends on the size of your network, count on Google if you don't have a large enough network on LinkedIn to bring fruitful results. In this case, you will not be able to send a quick InMail; you will need to send an email. This is the preferred method by job seekers that aren't looking to invest in LinkedIn Premium for the unlimited InMail allowance anyhow. (Only 3 InMail credits are included with the free subscription). It may sound difficult to find email addresses, but companies typically use the same email sequence for all their employees. Meaning, if I work at, let's say, PepsiCo, and my email is ldavis@pepsico.com, the hiring contact of Alicia Johnson's email is sure to be ajohnson@pepsico.com. Obviously, you will not always reach the right person, as sometimes the size of an organization makes this impossible. Also, you will not always receive a response; however, you increase your chances of an interview greatly by using the follow-up method.

Keep in mind that you can follow up on opportunities more than once if you have a different talking point each time. For instance, on the first round, you're letting them know that you've applied for the role and that you're available to answer any preliminary questions they may have. But on the next follow up, you're checking on the status of your application, or following up to see whether the position has been filled. The final follow up is for you to reiterate your interest in working for the company, and, assuming the role was filled, let them know that you want to be considered for future opportunities.

Connecting

The final thing that needs to be incorporated in your job search plan is networking and connecting. Spend just 15 to 20 minutes a day engaging on LinkedIn so that LinkedIn can do some of the work for you! The more active you are on the site, the more visible you become in the search database. When recruiters search keywords to look for potential candidates using LinkedIn's "Recruiter" tool, hundreds of pages of results pop up. The profiles that show up on the top pages are of people that are most active on the site. So, by engaging on LinkedIn, you're branding yourself and increasing your visibility at the same time. You could also consider publishing your own articles, but it's imperative that you comment on or share at least 2 to 3 posts per day. This alone will draw more attention to your profile, and get more recruiters to enlist you for job opportunities.

Final Thoughts

You need to focus on quality rather than quantity during your job search. You should spend no longer than 2 hours per day job hunting. Let us break down those 2 hours. Each week, you're applying for up to 15 positions according to a predetermined schedule. On two designated days out of the week, you are following up with hiring managers. You are also performing some daily activity on LinkedIn so it could bring job leads to you.

Bonus Tip: *Compile a target list of companies and prepare a script to cold market yourself to one contact each week.*

JOB SEARCH CHECKLIST

- ❏ Build your target company list
- ❏ Turn your job alerts on
- ❏ Research recruiters to partner with
- ❏ Post your resume to job boards

Daily:

- ❏ Complete 20 applications per week, or 4 applications per day.

Mondays & Thursdays:

- ❏ Follow up on prior week's submissions

LinkedIn Strategy:

- ❏ Engage with 2-3 posts per day
- ❏ Connect with 1 new person beneficial to your search each week.
- ❏ Send a Thank You to all new connections.

Sample weekly job search checklist

SAMPLE JOB SEARCH TRACKER

Title	Company	Pay Rate	Application Date	Response	Hiring Contact	Follow Up

Sample job tracker for recording, managing, and assessing your job search activity.

SAMPLE FOLLOW UP MESSAGE

Subject: Excited about the _____ opportunity!

Dear Hiring Manager*

My name is _____. I recently applied for the _____ opening, but I also wanted to personally introduce myself to you.

I have a strong background in _____, _____ and _____, and this appears to be an excellent match to the qualifications you are looking for!

I'm very interested in the opportunity and know that I can truly add value to your organization.

I realize that you may not be at the interview stage yet; however, I am more than happy to answer any preliminary questions you may have, and I can be reached at _____.

I'm looking forward to speaking with you about the role and my qualifications.

Sincerely, _____

Follow up with hiring managers on job opportunities after 5-7 days of applying.

"YOU CAN'T BUILD A REPUTATION ON WHAT YOU'RE GOING TO DO."

—CONFUCIUS

CHAPTER VI
SINK OR SAIL?
WORKING EFFECTIVELY WITH RECRUITERS

Job seekers have tons of questions about working with recruiters — questions concerning whether to even bother dealing with recruiters, or how to work effectively with them. The first thing to note about recruiters is, they are entirely focused on the employer's needs. Recruiters work for the hiring company, and not the job seeker. They only get paid upon making successful hires. So, they have no interest in candidates that don't fit the job requirements. In this chapter, we'll explore everything you need to know about recruiters and how to best manage these relationships.

What do recruiters do and how do they make money?

The job of a recruiter is twofold. Primarily, their responsibility is to source, screen, interview and place talent for companies. Their second job function is sales.

Why do several different recruiters work on the exact same role?

You might've noticed that two separate agencies have contacted you about the same job opening, or seen the exact position posted by a few different agencies on the job boards. Thus, recruiters stay "closest to the dollar" in their businesses. It all boils down to (1) who's representing the most favorable candidate at the time, (2) how strong, if any, the relationship is with the hiring company, and (3) if the company is really open to using an agency (and other factors). Companies usually avoid working with agencies to get around agency fees, unless the position is particularly hard to fill. In which case, for the perfect fit, the company will make the hire. Recruiters source through candidates until they find the best available person on the market (experience- and culture-wise) to win the competition.

What are recruiters trying to discover from the phone screen?

The phone screen usually determines how the relationship between a recruiter and job candidate will play out. *"We will submit your resume and if the company is interested, we'll reach out to you,"* is sometimes code talk that the recruiter isn't interested in pursuing a candidate any further. When recruiters have genuine interest in a candidate, they'll extend an invite for an in-person meeting, offer to show a formal job description, or establish clear communication from the onset. Generally, recruiters work to place candidates in positions they believe the candidate will be most successful. They usually go 'ghost' when they don't believe a person fits the necessary job requirements as outlined by their client.

Pro Tip: *If a recruiter ever ghosts you, make sure that you solicit feedback to increase your candidacy.*

What are some red flags for a poor match to recruiters?

Salary Demands

Recruiters use the salary question as a screening device to verify whether you fit the hiring company's needs and if you would make a good fit in the long-term (bad turnover/poor matches negatively impact the reputation with the client company).

Unemployment

Prepare to put a positive spin on your status if you're currently unemployed because recruiters sometimes see unemployment as a red flag. Like some employers, they assume you've either gotten lazy, or lost your skills. Think about in what way you're going to describe how you've been using your time during your break – or the events that led up to your exit from your last job.

Dishonesty

Recruiters filter out candidates they feel are being dishonest about gaps in employment, responsibilities, salary history, skill set, and other qualifications. They see the candidate's lack of honesty as a roadblock to establishing mutual trust.

What are recruiters looking for?

Recruiters look for candidates who match their clients' culture and work style. However, what's considered to be a good match can fall outside the scope of job responsibility, as sometimes recruiters take personality and appearance into account. They receive very specific instructions from the employer about what they're looking for.

Should people even bother to work with recruiters?

Yes! Good recruiters make excellent resources. Start thinking of recruiters as resources, but don't expect too much. Remember, recruiters do not work for the job candidate. They are in business to make money by closing talent for companies.

Here's a good set of questions to ask recruiters when pursing a relationship:

- *What kind of relationship do you have with the client?*
- *Were you retained for this position?*
- *Have you worked with this company before?*
- *How long have you been working on this assignment?*
- *Why is this position open?*
- *Have you presented any candidates yet to this client?*
- *Do you specialize in this industry?*

What are the top takeaways for working with recruiters?

1. Don't expect too much. It's nothing personal.
2. Take phone screens seriously, and conduct yourself as if you're speaking directly with the manager at the hiring company. First impressions are lasting.
3. Always solicit for feedback when things don't work out.
4. Stay well-versed on your explanation as to

employment gaps, separations, or unemployment.

5. Ask questions to get more insight into the relationship between the recruiter and hiring company.

"YOU ARE NEVER TOO OLD TO SET ANOTHER GOAL OR TO DREAM A NEW DREAM."

—C.S. LEWIS

CHAPTER VII
THE "RESUMES ARE DEAD" WAY:
NETWORKING TO THE OFFER

These days, it's who you know that can get you the job – and what you know that keeps you in the job. In today's job market, you must get out, get to know people, and treat every interaction as a potential opportunity. Remember that 4th of July cookout you got invited to? Perhaps someone might know of an opening that would fit your skill set. Study the field and endear yourself to some people that could help you get your foot in the door. Informational interviews, social media, professional events, and your primary network are all great methods to build and grow your professional network. Not only does networking accelerate the job search process, but job seekers can secure positions strictly through networking (without filling out a single application).

Informational Interviews

An informational interview is an informal conversation with someone who works in your field who could give you information and advice. It may feel awkward trying to arrange to talk with people you don't know. However, you'll find that some people enjoy taking a few moments to reflect on their careers and offer advice to people with an interest in their industries. There are so many benefits to informational interviews. For instance, you can uncover firsthand, relevant information about the realities of working in an industry or position. In fact, you may learn about new information that isn't easily found online. You can also learn about career paths that you never knew existed and get tips on how to prepare for or enter a given career. Or learn what it's like to work for a specific organization. Overall, informational interviews help you gain insight that can help you in writing your resume, interviewing and more.

Professional Events

Attending networking events is a great way to expand your network. This form of networking allows you to establish a more immediate connection because you get to spark a conversation right on the spot. Before you go to an event, ask yourself, "why am I going?" Then, come up with two desired outcomes — say, meeting three new people or getting one new job lead. Target social and professional networking events, or events hosted by professional associations within your industry. A few days after the event, send follow-up emails to anyone you met that you'd like to continue networking with. Make sure that you personalize your emails, letting each person know you enjoyed meeting them and mentioning something that you talked about.

Primary Network

It's time to contact everyone in your network, including past colleagues, friends, college friends, clients, or bosses. Draft an email sharing that you're on the market and that you're enlisting their help. And, be specific about what you're asking for. Is it job leads or postings? Informational interviews? New contacts? All the above? Your email should include all the details they need to help you: your current position and company, the length of time you've been there, and what you're looking for and where!

NETWORKING SCRIPTS

Use these scripts to start networking with past colleagues, classmates, or clients – or to request informational interviews.

Subject: Touching Base

Hi Person,

I hope all is well!

We worked together at _____/studied together at _____/ met in _____'s course.

I'm reaching out to you because I'm currently on the job market and wanted to see if
you knew about any potential opportunities.

For the past year, I've worked as a _____, and I'm looking to obtain a position as _____.

Could we connect?

It's no pressure, but I do hope to hear back from you.

Kind regards,
Your Name

NETWORKING SCRIPTS
INFORMATIONAL INTERVIEWS

Hi Person,

It's nice to meet you. I noticed that you worked at _____ (or that you work in _____), and I was wondering if I could borrow a few minutes of your time to talk about your experiences.

It's no pressure, but I do hope to hear back from you.

Kind Regard,
Your Name

NETWORKING SCRIPTS
INTRODUCTION TO RECRUITERS

Dear Recruiter,

I hope this message finds you well.

My name is _____, and I just wanted to personally introduce myself to you.

I have a strong background in _____, _____ and _____. For the past __ years, I've worked as a _____ at _____, and I'm specifically looking to apply my skills in a career as _____.

I'm reaching out to see if you know about any available opportunities. If so, I would be happy to forward you my credentials so that we could discuss any positions that you're working on that may be a good fit.

I'm looking forward to speaking with you about the role and my qualifications.

Sincerely,
Your Name

"KEEP YOUR EYES ON THE STARS, AND YOUR FEET ON THE GROUND."

—THEODORE ROOSEVELT

CHAPTER VIII
DESTINATION LINKEDIN:
LEVERAGING LINKEDIN IN YOUR JOB SEARCH

LinkedIn is by far the most valuable social networking tool for job seekers. Use it correctly, and it could well help you build successful networking connections with ideal employers. If you are in search of your dream career, you are missing out on a wealth of available opportunities if you are skipping out on everything LinkedIn has to offer. LinkedIn is where you'll find the professionals that are most interested in your skills, experience or value. Today, there are over 3 million businesses on LinkedIn, providing access to a network of over 200 million professionals around the world. There are easily over 420 million users on LinkedIn, and the site is still growing daily. This means that your presence on LinkedIn could pay real dividends. You should have these two goals with LinkedIn: (1) to be discoverable by your ideal employers, and (2) to attract and build networking connections that are meaningful to your purpose of being on the site. But, this all begins with a profile.

THE PROFILE

The first thing you want to do is turn off the notification to share your profile updates with your network. After reading this material, your profile may go under major construction, and the last thing you want to do is alert your network of every single change you make to your profile. To do this, you need to:

Go to Settings & Privacy > Privacy Tab > Sharing Profile Edits > select "No".

Since you're competing with over 420 million other

professionals, you need to build a killer LinkedIn profile to stand out above people that bring similar value as you do. Your profile is the first meeting of your brand to your key audience. The content is your profile. It is YOU people are looking to learn more about, so your profile content must be consistent with who you are in the real world. It should inspire people to want to contact you and learn more about your capabilities. As you're creating your profile, check out other profiles for artistic emphasis and inspiration. Now, let's discuss how you can create a killer profile.

Your Headshot

One basic rule to building a successful LinkedIn profile is by using a professional headshot. Although highly recommended, it isn't exactly necessary to hire a professional photographer for your profile picture. All you need is a picture with good lighting that captures your best angles, shows your entire face and displays a professional image. However, refrain from using any pictures of yourself holding a coffee cup – or selfies. Send a friendly message in your picture, and, importantly, SMILE. Don't be afraid to show your quirks.

Your Headline

After your profile picture, the next thing your viewers will notice is your headline. LinkedIn automatically defaults this 120-character headline to your most recent position. But, that doesn't do you justice to describe who you really are and what you do. You could really give focus to recruiters by using all the space available. After reading your headline, your audience should know instantly why you're valuable to them. Your headline is an area the search engine rates as key in establishing your profile's ranking in the search database, too. It should capture your target position and most critical skills. You can even add a quirky twist to your headline to connect with your viewers–if it speaks to what you do/who you are. To get some ideas, use the advanced search to view people that work in your same role or industry.

Profile Summary

Unlike the 120-character space for your headline, the summary section allows for much more flexibility for you to include all the right information that your key audience needs for better discoverability. Take full advantage of this space. You will grow your summary gradually; however, while starting out you can use the first few lines or so of your resume profile. Your summary is simply a brief digest of the key skills and experience that your viewers are looking for in someone to hire. If possible, continue to repeat keywords in your summary to further increase your discoverability. You could also use a call-to-action to instantly let people know how they can reach you.

Work Experience

When completing the work experience section, don't just include titles, companies, and dates. Be sure to also include your job details, which you could paste directly from your resume. You make yourself more visible when keywords are repeated throughout your headline, summary, and the details of your work history.

Recommendations

Gather recommendations from colleagues, business partners, or coworkers to increase your brand's credibility. Recommendations also help to improve your discoverability in the search database. These may prove difficult to obtain, but when you commit the act, people are more apt to return the favor. So, simply start a list of five people or so who could write a recommendation on your behalf, go to their profiles, and write recommendations for them. Then, ask them to return the favor. Recommendations give your profile more appeal and demonstrates your ability to work with others as well as your quality of work.

Pro Tip: Include samples of your work on your profile to give your viewers instant access or insight into your work style – including websites you helped create, projects, and PDFs.

Contact Information

You don't want to make it hard for people to be able to reach you, so complete all the elements of the contact section by listing your email address, phone number, and social media handles. Also, create a vanity URL for your profile to establish your brand.

Pro Tip: *Remove any funny characters that may be included in your profile's URL (www.linkedin.com/in/lakrisha-davis-* ~~827b00135/~~*).*

SEARCH ENGINE OPTIMIZATION

If you've followed all the prompts to create a killer profile correctly, as outlined above, your profile should already be optimized for the maximum discoverability in the search database. You should have already repeated the keywords, skills, and experiences relevant to your field in these areas:

1. *Headline*
2. *Summary*
3. *Work Experience and Job Titles*
4. *Recommendations*

Now, go back to your profile and make sure that these sections include your most critical titles/skills/credentials/experience/keywords that are necessary to your value proposition.

Besides your profile content, there are a few other tricks you could use to further optimize your visibility. Let's look at the Projects and Publications sections as examples to promote SEO. You can list case studies, projects, eBooks, articles, etc. in these areas. They can be used in the title of the project or publication and can also be added in a description to maximize keyword exposure.

In addition to projects, you need endorsements. The more skills endorsements you obtain, the higher you rank for those keywords in the search database. To get more endorsements, you could endorse someone first and ask them to return the favor. LinkedIn allows you to list up to 50 skills. However, by listing fewer skills, you can get more endorsements for each skill, which promotes greater discoverability.

GROW YOUR NETWORK

LinkedIn allows you to connect with a bank of over 200 million people you wouldn't otherwise be able to connect with. The site recommends you to only connect with people you know personally or professionally. And to this day, LinkedIn still takes this stance. However, the site's users have dramatically changed how they use the site, and it's becoming more and more common for people to make connections with new people outside of their network. There's still a huge population of users that turn down requests from strangers. But they run the risk of limiting their networking power considerably. Sometimes, total strangers can do more for you than people already in your network. In this section, we'll explore ways you could grow your professional network on LinkedIn.

Special Interest Groups

Your primary goal of joining LinkedIn groups is to attract people that can most benefit from your core skill-sets. Remember, the site only allows you to directly message people (without using any InMail credits) if they are one of your LinkedIn connections, or if you share an interest. Being a member of the same group as someone else qualifies you as having a shared interest. So, you'll have access to all members of the group. There's a plethora of special-interest groups you could join to find the people you're looking for. LinkedIn allows you to join up to 50. You could join groups where recruiters and other job seekers hang out. Focus on groups where you can pinpoint the people most likely to help advance your job search or industry knowledge.

To make connections within these groups, you need to increase your visibility by commenting on, "liking," and adding value to the discussions. You could also share your own original content to the groups, or other content you find valuable to the community. Once you make a connection with someone in the group by way of exchanging in some conversation or complimenting their content, this creates a safe ground for you to take it a step further by asking to connect.

Making Posts

One of your primary goals on the LinkedIn site is to become more discoverable to your key audience. Like special-interest groups, you increase your visibility by adding value to and commenting on different conversations or articles started by other LinkedIn users. Set a goal to do this 2 to 3 times a day, and you'll instantly notice more profile views, connection requests, and people wanting to learn more about your background. Another surefire way to increase your visibility is to publish your own posts. Make your audience fall in love with your personality through engagement, questions, and value. And, you don't always need to reinvent the wheel. You could share content written by other people with the community. Just keep in mind - LinkedIn isn't Twitter. It's not okay to post 5 or 6 times a day. Also, try to keep self-promotion to a minimum.

Pro Tip: *Be on the lookout for posts with tons of engagement. Follow/connect with those authors to merge with their networks. You could also write your own articles, or share your blogs.*

Advanced Search

Using the advanced search, you can search to find meaningful relationships on LinkedIn. You can search for job titles, companies, industries, geographic locations, and keywords and get thousands of results within seconds. Once you find people you want to make a connection with, send them a connection request with an added note — not the generic one LinkedIn has prepared by default. By adding a note, you increase your chances of a successful connection. After the connection request is accepted, you can send a follow-up message to thank them for the connection or start up a chat using a conversation opener.

"MOTIVATION IS WHAT GETS YOU STARTED. HABIT IS WHAT KEEPS YOU GOING."

—JIM RYUN

CHAPTER IX
CRUISING THE INTERVIEW:
BECOMING AN INTERVIEWING PRO

When you've successfully mastered writing your cover letter and resume and are finally getting called for interviews, it's about time to understand how to succeed in the interview process. The interview process is another barrier that could prevent you from getting the job offer. Preparing for the interview can sometimes feel nerve-wracking since you really have no idea what you're preparing for, what questions you'll get asked, or what the interviewer will throw your way.

So how does one truly prepare themselves for this? The answer is simple: companies don't invest in potential;

they invest in candidates that best match the role both skillset- and culture-wise. In this chapter, we focus on the most critical interviewing tips—regardless of the position being applied for.

Research the Organization, Interviewer and Job Description

Successful interviewing begins with a solid foundation of knowledge on the part of the candidate, so you must always conduct research on the company to be able to: (1) speak to what the company does, (2) describe how you could contribute to organizational goals, and (3) explain why you support the company's mission. You'd also want to be able to relate to the interviewer on a personal level by learning about his personal background, too.

By studying the job description, you familiarize yourself with your skill sets, relevant experience, and achievements that are most relevant to the job details. Rehearse what you've written down on your resume, and practice talking about what you bring to the table in a consistent manner (with proper body language).

Always Be Prepared to Answer the Common Questions

Another key to interview success is preparing the responses to the questions you'll get asked. The tricky thing with this is, you sometimes don't know what sort of interview style you will face. But you can, however, look to online resources, such as Glassdoor, to read about other candidates' interview experiences along with questions they've been asked. While some interviewers prefer an informal approach (where you're likely to ask most of the questions), others already have in mind what job-specific questions they'll ask you. There are a few questions job seekers should always have in their back pockets and be ready to answer:

1. *What is missing from your employer - or why do you want to leave your current position?*

   It's fine to be authentic with your response. But, stay away from cookie-cutter responses like "looking for a challenge" or "more room for advancement." Instead, focus on the direction the company is heading and how this is conducive to your career goals/passions. (i.e. this company is innovation-driven and your current company isn't set up to allow you to make the impact that you'd like to make in the field.) It's fine to be authentic with your response. But, stay away from cookie-cutter responses like "looking for a challenge" or "wanting more room for advancement." Instead, focus on the direction the company is headed and why this is conducive to your career goals or passions.

2. **Tell about the time when...**

Be prepared for any requests for real-world examples—also known as behavioral interview questions. Your best bet is to have 1 to 3 stories prepared and ready to go for your interview. Here are a few big ones you should make sure to have in your collection. They're general enough that they can be used for a variety of questions, but specific enough that the person asking will feel like he or she's getting a good, solid, detail-filled response:

- When You Overcame a Challenge
- When You Made a Mistake
- When You Solved a Problem

Also consider bringing along a portfolio to the interview (if applicable) with excerpts from past performance evaluations, pictures of workflows that you created, evidence of any certifications or awards, or recommendations from colleagues.

3. *What are your strengths and weaknesses?*

   Stick with a response that is a true weakness (because you want to answer the questions, of course) but could also complement your work ethic/passion. Be sure to reinforce why this is a strength career-wise but is a weakness personally to you. For instance, "I'm a workaholic who can always be counted on to get the job done; however, my personal life suffers."

4. *Tell me about yourself.*

   Master this question for every interview by

developing an elevator pitch. As you begin to put together your elevator pitch, nail down the best way to describe your field and the type of job you're pursuing. Remember, this speech is about you, but you will need to tailor the pitch to them. Be mindful that the people listening to your speech will have their ears tuned to what's in it for them, so focus your message on their needs. Your elevator pitch should address who you are, what you do, why you're the best, and your goals.

Let's formulate my elevator pitch, for example:

Who are you? A Career Coach, Success Mentor, and Speaker.

What do you do? Help ambitious people all over the world navigate Corporate America to create the lives and careers they've always dreamed of.

Why are you the best? Not only do I have a bird's eye view into the hiring climate as a former HR professional, but I've had personal success in landing my dream career and increasing by salary by over 60% once as a job seeker.

What is your goal? I want to continue building upon my craft and help as many career professionals as I possibly can get the careers that they love and deserve.

Read my 30-60 second elevator pitch here:
"I'm a Career Coach, Success Mentor, and Speaker. I help ambitious people all over the world navigate Corporate America to create the lives and careers they've always dreamed of. What sets me apart from other coaches is that I not only have a bird's eye view into the hiring climate as a former HR professional, but as a job seeker I've also had personal success in landing my dream career and increasing by salary by over 60%. My goal is to continue building upon my craft and help as many career professionals as possible get jobs that they love and deserve."

Now, it's your turn!

- State who you are:
- Say what you do based on the job description:
- Tell what makes you the best!
- Let them know your goal:

5. *Why do you want to work for the company? Or, what do you know about the company?*

   When delivering your response to this question, you need to speak from passion and sound believable. Research and find out something unique about the company that you really love (mission/values/culture/offerings/community involvement) and tie this into your response. Consider how the company's mission aligns with your personal mission.

6. *What are your salary requirements?*

   You don't need to specify salary requirements as it is too early in the process to allow yourself to be identified by a specific salary demand. Employers often use this inquiry as a screening device, so you certainly don't want to give off too much information too soon. You risk getting eliminated from the candidate pool if your number exceeds their budget. Or, you risk underquoting yourself if you're unaware of the level of enthusiasm that the employer has about retaining you. Be sure to utilize online resources available to get a sense of what they're paying for the seat.

There are a couple of ways you can approach the salary question, and this entirely depends upon your own personal salary expectations. For instance, if you have a deal breaker salary in mind, meaning you will not accept a job paying less than $80,000, for example, when the salary question comes up, let them know your number so that you don't waste your time. However, if you are open to negotiating based on the opportunity, let them know this as well. If you're not comfortable with sharing your current salary details, let them know that you rather focus on the value that you bring:

"I don't feel comfortable sharing this information and instead would like to focus on the value that I can bring to your organization. I will say that I am looking to make this a big move in my career in terms of responsibility and compensation and that I'm hoping to make something within the range of $XX,XXX - $XX,XXX. I am willing to negotiate depending on the opportunity."

Make Good First Impressions

A cardinal rule of successful interviewing is to make a good first impression. Create a strong impression by bringing extra copies of your resume, dressing to impress (in a blue or grey suit), shaking hands firmly and making good eye contact. Employers often observe to see how job applicants treat staff members as well, so be sure to warmly greet everyone you encounter in the office. You should always arrive at your interview at least 15-20 minutes prior to the scheduled time, as there's no excuse for arriving late to an interview. Consider driving a practice route to the interview location to make sure you get there on time.

Be Authentic, Upbeat and Confident

Once the interview starts, focus on delivering quality responses that showcase your skills and experience, and that also fits with the job and employer. But, it's important to keep your responses focused, short and to the point; at the same token, it should show your personality and confidence.

Ask Great Questions

Key to closing an interview successfully is asking great questions about the job, hiring manager, and the opportunity. Ask questions to show your curiosity about the organization and to get a better picture of how it would feel working there. If it feels organic, feel free to ask questions as they come to mind. Keeping them in the back of your mind until the end might distract you during.

Always Follow Up with a Thank You

Finally, within 24 hours of interviewing with the company, follow up with a note to thank the interviewer for their time either via email or in a handwritten note.

SAMPLE THANK YOU NOTE

Dear Hiring Manager*

Thank you very much for allowing me the opportunity to interview for the position of Position Title* at Company Name*.

It was a pleasure meeting with you, and I truly enjoyed learning more about the role and the company. After our meeting, I feel confident that my skills and experiences are a great match for this opportunity.

Again, thank you for your consideration.

Please let me know if you have any questions or concerns or need more information.

Sincerely,
Your Name*

Thank the interviewer(s) for the time they spent meeting with you about the position within 24 hours after the interview.

SAMPLE INTERVIEW QUESTIONS

When the inevitable, "So, do you have any questions for us?" part of the interview comes, choose from this list to make sure you've covered all your bases.

Questions about the opportunity:

1. What are the common career paths in this department?
2. What metrics or goals will my performance be evaluated against?
3. Where have successful employees previously in this position progressed to?
4. What does a typical day look like?
5. What types of skills is the team missing that you're looking to fill with a new hire?
6. What are the biggest challenges that someone in this position would face?
7. Thinking back to people you've seen do this work previously, what differentiated the ones who were good from the ones who were great at it?

8. What are you hoping for the new hire to accomplish within the first 90 days of employment?
9. How will you know that you've made the right hiring decision?

Questions to ask the interviewer:

10. What's your timeline for next steps?
11. Is there anything else I can provide you with that would be helpful?
12. What gets you most excited about the company's future?
13. What's your favorite part about working here?
14. Has your role changed since you've been here?

"AN OBSTACLE MAY BE EITHER A STEPPING STONE OR A STUMBLING BLOCK."

—UNKNOWN

CHAPTER X:
BUMPS IN THE ROAD:
LESSONS ABOUT AGE DISCRIMINATION

Dozens of job seekers feel plagued by employment discrimination. But first, what is employment discrimination? It is the basis of hiring decisions on race, color, religion, sex or national origin. In retrospect, when I first started my coaching business I was certain that I'd be working mostly with millennials because:

- Age plays a factor in experience level, and experience outweighs education in today's job market; and
- Stereotypes exist about the work ethics of millennial workers and their "sense of entitlement".

Statistics even show that on average, millennials change jobs 5 to 6 times within 2-3 years. These figures also reflect that millennials are the least engaged group in the workplace. I figured this generation would find coaching most critical. But, what is interesting was the pattern of Generation X workers soliciting for coaching — complaining of being unable to find satisfying work specifically due to their age.

Ever since *Title VII of the 1964 Civil Rights Act* passed into law, it has made employment discrimination illegal against someone because of, amongst other things, their age. Despite the laws, discrimination hasn't been completely eradicated. The fact of the matter is - hiring managers would never openly tell a job seeker to their face that they think they're too old. Rather, the curse of discrimination is most often silent.

Here are some ugly truths:

1. We live in a youth-centered culture, and your appearance may not appear as youthful as it once did.

2. The higher you climb the professional ladder, employers assume you require more money — which will ultimately cost the company more.

3. Certain adult learning theories assert that seasoned workers are "know-it-alls" or may potentially pose problems for management.

4. They assume adult learners are not as current with applications of technology.

While age discrimination is totally unjust and illegal, it's easy to point the finger of blame and slowly resign to diminished horizons. As this form of discrimination has nothing to do with a candidate's ability to perform the job, it's best to fight back with experience, understanding and with the street smarts you've accumulated through the years.

How are employers getting away with it, you ask? The issue is that when candidates don't get hired, they rarely find out the candidate who got the offer. This makes it incredibly challenging to prove to a court of law that the candidate was less fit for the job than you, especially when you don't really understand the intimate details of their background.

Here are some ways for job seekers to beat age discrimination:

1. Make sure your resume is age discrimination proof. Hiring managers can just guess an applicant's age based on how they're presented on their resume. Here's what to do:

    - **If you have tons of job experience, don't list all of it.** It can give an idea about the age group you belong in. Use "Additional Experience" to state relevant work history that's older than 10-12 years and list the position and title only. Stick with job experience that's most relevant to the job description. Meaning, if that only includes your last three jobs then leave all that other stuff off (it's probably irrelevant by now anyway).

    - **Don't list graduation dates.** Although people continue/pursue an education at all age levels, some employers still think they know whether you're Generation X or Y based on college graduation dates.

- **Do away with old school techniques:** (1) Microsoft templates; (2) stating 'references upon request' on your resume; or (3) using objective statements.

- **Get rid of email accounts such as AOL, Yahoo!, etc.** if you use them (they signal you've got to be 40 or over) and sign up for a Gmail account.

2. Master the question of age on the interview

   An interviewer may be bold enough to ask directly what age category you fall in. Although questions concerning age can typically be considered illegal, this sometimes doesn't stop the interviewer from asking. Regardless, it wouldn't advance your candidacy to take offense to the question, so let's explore ways you can better answer this:

   "It's interesting that you should ask. I just turned 49, and this gives me years of experience

doing exactly what's demanded of the job. In my years of experience, I've been exposed to all sorts of situations and environments. I have also made my share of mistakes on someone else's dime, and have learned from those mistakes greatly (Smile). The greatest benefit of my experience level of all is that _____."

(Fill in the blank with benefit statements relevant to the job).

3. Manage your appearance

   Your personal appearance has a huge impact on fighting age discrimination. We live in a youth-centered culture where the appearance of clothes, hair, and skin can say a lot about your ability to fit in the work culture. You need to do everything you can to maintain the vibrancy of your appearance..

4. Seek opportunities at smaller companies

   Smaller companies are more than likely growth-focused, whereas larger companies may aim to cut costs. As a seasoned worker, you can leverage your maturity as someone who may serve as a great benefit because you have likely encountered and solved problems before that exist in the organization. In this type of culture, hiring managers may likely see your wisdom and depth of experience very valuable.

Although illegal, employment discrimination still occurs. While you can't control it from happening, you can certainly give it your best fight!

"IF YOU CAN DREAM IT, YOU CAN DO IT."

—WALT DISNEY

CHAPTER XI:
HITTING A GOLDMINE:
NEGOTIATING THE OFFER

Many job seekers shy away from asking for more money. Some of us are afraid to ask, and some of us have the courage to ask, but will stop short of asking for what we really want or what we're truly worth. But in any case, you're missing out on more than just money; you're putting your long-term earning potential at stake. If you've ever stopped before negotiating your true market value, remember that in today's market, companies expect candidates to negotiate. They are usually assigned a specific budget to pay for a position (i.e. $60,000 - $70,000), depending on the candidate. You don't know whether the company has offered you the maximum dollar, or saved a little "wiggle room" in case you decide to negotiate. But in most cases, you can rest assured that they've saved wiggle room for negotiations. So, always try and negotiate your offer. Negotiation is a conversation where the goal is to reach an agreement with someone whose interests are not perfectly aligned with yours. So, unless you ask, you may be leaving money on the table.

When initiating the conversation, start out by simply asking whether the offer is open for negotiations. They will let you know then, or they may have to ask the person with authority and get back to you. If they tell you no, they are flat out saying that the offer is non-negotiable. Then, if you'd like, you can let them know that you just wanted to ask and can redeem yourself and say that you're still interested in the opportunity. Or, if they say yes, that's your opportunity to negotiate. Now you can plead your case. Why should you get paid more? Do you have another offer on the table? Did you just pursue some type of education requirement that gives you the competitive advantage? Do you possess leadership qualities outside of the scope of the position that gives you leverage? Expect these questions (or something similar) to be asked once the discussions of salary negotiations get underway. Thinking about these potential inquiries will better prepare you for that conversation overall!

MOCKUP NEGOTIATIONS DIALOGUE

NON-NEGOTIABLE JOB OFFER:

Candidate: "Mary, thank you so much for your offer. I'm excited about the potential of working at the company because **the role seems like the perfect challenge I'm looking for, and I also love the company's work culture.** However, I did have a different number in mind as far as salary is concerned, and was wondering if the offer is at all negotiable?"

Interviewer: "Andrea, I'm sorry, but the offer is non-negotiable."

Candidate: "I appreciate your consideration, Mary. I would not have felt comfortable without at least asking, but I will accept your offer. I'll have a signed offer emailed to you right away.

MOCKUP NEGOTIATIONS DIALOGUE

NEGOTIABLE JOB OFFER:

Candidate: "Mary, thank you so much for your offer. I'm excited about the potential of working at the company because the **role seems like the perfect challenge I'm looking for, and I also love the company's work culture.** However, I did have a different number in mind as far as salary is concerned, and was wondering if the offer is at all negotiable?"

Interviewer: "Hi, Andrea. Yes, I'd be willing to negotiate your offer. What number did you have in mind?"

Candidate: "Great! Well, I did receive another offer, but I'm more excited about working at your company. They did offer me $80,000, as opposed to the $70,000 your company has offered. I would feel comfortable accepting your offer if it's within the range of $80-85 thousand dollars.

Interviewer: "Thanks, Andrea! I'll review your counter offer and let you know our decision right away."

ACKNOWLEDGMENT

I am thankful for the job that I hated. I am also thankful for my stint in working in the recruiting industry. Had I never hated my job, I would not have gotten serious about learning the strategies to land my dream career. And, my job in recruiting exposed me to a ton about the hiring market... the upsides, glass ceiling barriers, and so much more that I can share with the world.

SPECIAL THANKS

I want to send a special thanks to those who have contributed to my success in writing this book, and have also taken a vested interest in my personal and career success. Each one of you have helped me in different ways — through your knowledge, shared resources, or emotional support. Though the list could go on and on, I will take my best stab...

Thank you to my family, friends, and colleagues:

- *A. Ford*
- *A. Humphrey*
- *A. Adkins*
- *C. Hawthrone*
- *E. Venable*
- *T. Verseane*

And so many more. Thank you for everything!

ABOUT THE AUTHOR

Meet your guide, Lakrisha Davis – Career Coach, Success Mentor, Speaker – who helps ambitious job seekers all over the world navigate the corporate landscape to create the life and career they've always dreamed of.

Lakrisha has over 10+ years of combined experiences working in HR, recruiting, and compliance, supporting Fortune 500 clients like Fiat Chrysler (FCA US), Ford Motor Company, RR Donnelley & Sons, Groupon, Deere & Company, Sears Holding Co., Mercedes-Benz, Discover Card Services, Bank of America, and Allstate. From obtaining an MBA in Human Resources Management; to getting a bird's eye view into the hiring climate; to leveraging the strategies and philosophies acquired through my corporate career; and networking and connecting with successful women – she has mentored and coached hundreds of professionals out of unfulfilling jobs and into the careers they love.

www.ingramcontent.com/pod-product-compliance
Lightning Source LLC
LaVergne TN
LVHW041632070426
835507LV00008B/580